I0879478

WORLD WITHOUT MAPS

Poems pass from hand to hand,
firemen's buckets
to keep the heart at bay.

Praise for *World Without Maps*

'Geraldine Mitchell writes with such sophistication and élan that it is difficult to think that this is a first collection. Her special gift is a description of the illusory veils of Maya that all our lives are made of again and again. This added to an extraordinary gift for image and metaphor which makes a weekend plane trip abroad 'the well-worn arc of a patinated shuttle/plying back and forth to weave our lives/together. Darning holes' ('Flight Patterns'). Geraldine Mitchell is a very careful observer and listener. She always was: 'But my eyes saw, my ears heard,/my nose picked up/the layered scent of adult talk' ('The Invisible Girl'). This manuscript is a distillation of all those years of picking up layered scents. It is a real find and a thoughtful read. It brims with possibilities'

– Nuala Ní Dhomhnaill

'These are the poems of a considered and considering intelligence, surefooted, meditative and clear. One is in the presence of a clear-eyed sensibility that considers, but does not judge, human fallibility [...] The language of these poems is succinct, the imagery crisp and the poet has the confidence to allow the images and rhythms to work their chemistry upon us without too much commentary. In the best of these poems we are left with an image which resonates and opens out into mystery – something which is at the core of the poetic'

– Moya Cannon and Theo Dorgan,
Judges' Report, The Patrick Kavanagh Award, 2008

World Without Maps

Geraldine Mitchell

ARLEN
HOUSE

World Without Maps

is published in 2012 by
Arlen House
an imprint of Arlen Publications Ltd
42 Grange Abbey Road
Baldoyle
Dublin 13
Ireland
Phone/Fax: 353 86 8207617
Email: arlenhouse@gmail.com

Distributed internationally by
Syracuse University Press
621 Skytop Road, Suite 110
Syracuse, NY 13244–5290
Phone: 315–443–5534/Fax: 315–443–5545
Email: supress@syr.edu

1st edition, 2011
ISBN 978–1–85132–020–2, paperback

2nd edition, 2012
ISBN 978–1–85132–043–1, paperback
ISBN 978–1–85132–053–0, hardback

Front Cover Image ¦ 'Mad Fish', Karen Papacek
www.papacek.com
Back Cover Image ¦ Photograph of sculpture
'Protection', Leanne Mullen

Contents

Acknowledgements

Acknowledgements are due to the editors of the following, in which some of these poems, or versions of them, first appeared: *Cyphers, Drogheda Writers 2, Moloch, Poetry Ireland Review, Poetry Salzburg, Southword, Stand, The SHOp, The Stinging Fly, The Interpreter's House, The Irish Times, The Stony Thursday Book, The Sunday Tribune.*

A version of the poem 'Fell' appeared in the anthology *Present Tense,* edited by Macdara Woods and Jim Vaughan (Mayo County Council, 2006).

A version of 'The Trees in Her Head' won first prize in the Amergin 2007 Creative Writing Awards.

'Lull' appeared in the Oxfam 2009 Calendar.

Thanks are due to Mayo County Council for a bursary to Annaghmakerrig and to the Heinrich Böll Association for a residency at the Cottage. Very special thanks go to Nuala Ní Dhomhnaill for her belief in my work at a critical time; to Joan McBreen for her support and encouragement; to Jean Tuomey and the Castlebar 'Writing on Tuesdays' group; and last, but far from least, to poets Michelle O'Sullivan, Peggie Gallagher, Aoife Casby and Ann Joyce.

For Neil, Lisa and Yann

World Without Maps

Orbit

For three million euro
– give or take –
you can see the sun rise
eighteen times a day.
It's true. I heard it on the radio.
And where would that
leave the moon?

With us, making our descent to Jo'burg,
a lost eyelash,
brittle and new,
snagged on the pre-dawn's lurid
lightshow, orange, green
and deepest blue.

Or waiting for us back up north,
old and wall-eyed, watching
as we slide under water into Paris,
rock pools gleaming.

If you travel fast enough
you can live in darkness
all your life,
or in too much light.

Ultrasound

Deep in the pockets of my memory
are coins rubbed smooth from fingering,
stories I have hoarded, guarded
from the corruption of sharing.

The night we spent in the one-room house
in Kabylia, after broad beans and buttermilk
from a single dish. You in the big bed with him.
The honour.

Me and his wife on the floor.
How in the night she wrapped her arms around me,
and from behind the fortress of her belly
her child tapped messages on my back.

Bunlough Point

Sometimes light thickens
on winter afternoons,
drenching the air with radiance,
sharpening the focus,
picking out each crevice, every crease
in the black shore rocks.

It must be a painter's dream
to catch that intensity:
the honey tints and tarry blacks,
the blues of infants' eyes,
the snow-capped waves.

To capture the burnished air
before day ends.

Latent

If you want to make a carving
of a bear, said Henry Moore,
just take everything away
that isn't bear.

Michelangelo had the knack.
He chipped away at everything
that wasn't loss, until what was left
was a mother holding her dead son.

Bernini took from metamorphic rock
all that was not tensile give and texture:
imprint of fingers on resisting flesh,
folds of cloth, the leg beneath,
the ecstasy of orgasm in half-closed eyes.

Through white silk, hard as ice,
truth emerges by elimination,
in bloodless bodies, life.

The Suitcase of Bees

She brought it with her everywhere,
its silver, dimpled surface effervescent
with the whirr of wings within. In public
she would spread her skirt's thick folds
to mute the angry drone, paint a smile
across her face, hope no-one would notice.

Once inside her own four walls
the vibrations grew so shrill
she held her head and hummed.
The ambulance crew was gentle
as they led her owl-eyed through the gates,
bees still rustling taffeta in her head.

The case was silent, a ruse
in sly collusion with the doctor
who swore she was an expert,
knew all there was to know
of stings and swarms, their stridency,
how to outface the queen.

They built a wooden beehive,
surrounded it with lemon balm, sweet basil, mint.
And now, except for mild tinnitus, she is calm.

EARTHED

I would like my life to be
a winter vegetable garden,
an unfenced strip at the edge
of a fallow field. Stout leeks
standing shoulder to shoulder,
brassicas, blousy and generous,
silver artichokes, spiky, aloof.

I would like to have the good sense to know
the nature of winter and welcome it,
my roots clawed deep to steady me
against the *tramontane* or even snow,
relishing the chance
to comb the dormant subsoil.

I would like people passing
on their way to the supermarket
in their centrally heated cars
to be taken unawares: a warm kitchen,
a lifted lid, rich steam rushing past
their cheeks; to assault them with a memory
they did not know was there.

Geometry

Not-quite-tangential lines near-missing:
the bus that almost knocked him down,
the bullet with her name misspelt on it,
the one that got away.

We play with death to keep it
distracted, make it turn away
from the child on the window ledge,
the falling tree,
the ticking clock.

Quiescent

after seeing Clonycavan Man *and* Old Croghan Man
at the National Museum, Dublin

I

Your neck's wrung round for one last look,
one mean stare at your executioners,
one they'd remember, a look to pierce
their hearts the way they planned to pin you
to the soggy depths, make sure
you'd not be back to haunt them.

The summer was coming to an end,
the crops were in, days shortening,
your henna-ed hair fixed into place
with best French resin, backcombed
to a prehistoric Mohican in celebration.
You were no ordinary rocker.

II

Tall as a Dinka, old at twenty-five,
your strong arms swing in graceful dance.
Now less than half a man, your long legs lost,
your headless torso is all that's left,
a child's bolero crumpled from the wash.

Intimate as an arm across my pillow at first light,
I study the pores of your umber skin,
examine every last hair's socket,
follow the veins roped round your knuckles,
wonder at the tailored nails, your unclenched hands.

Funeral

The prayers ended in a scattering of words,
potatoes spilled on a wooden floor.

In my silence I felt absence,
a single stone in a cleft tree.

The prayers ended in a scattering, I walked
right as they turned left. My feet unheard.

Mirror, Mirror

Il arrive toujours ce moment
où l'on ne se reconnaît plus
dans le miroir
à force de vivre sans reflet
– Dany Laferrière, *L'énigme du retour*

A net of starlings skims an oval patch of sky
where water pools the flooded field,
sifted greys and blue, fistfuls of feather
broadcast where no eye watches,
simple pleasure of the air.

The silence is dark.

I cannot see myself.

Mirror, mirror on the wall,
is there anyone here at all?

My eyes are sealed.
Mute surfaces glaze
deep and still.

Plate glass tracks me in the mall,
throws me back onto myself,
a stranger, no other eyes
to take me in.

Leaning over water
I want to drink the image dry.
One false move and I am crazed,
the surface cracked.

I plunge headfirst
into the echo of my loss.

The valley lies silent,
the well drinks down
my shout.
A voice whispers
You've reached the place where nothing will come back.

Snowflakes stumble
from a bruised and swollen sky,
paw the trees' bare bones, the glass;
I fall through the feathered threshold,

night's watchful secret.

* *The moment inevitably comes when, having lived for so long without seeing your reflected image, you no longer recognise yourself in the mirror.*

LULL

If I could walk into a painting
it would be this one. Slip
into silence and looking back
see your mouth moving,
let the glass hold me, the sun
unpack me pore by pore.

In here, no breath. No movement
over the green-washed fields
or the woods beyond.
No sound but the soft hiss of sand
falling, falling through fingers,
dry ruffling of feathers.

But the earth turns,
air begins to dart and puff,
spring corn flattens; cell by cell,
gravity bent, blades are sucked
into movement; trees sway, leaning,
longing for the threatening storm.

Dams Hold Back Water

The sea is going nowhere
beside Belmullet pier,
it puckers mean and grey,
slaps the low wall all day
making me see

how water needs to flow
somewhere, to fall as rain,
run down a mountainside, or
be the river we step in
and out of. I remember

one March Sunday
watching a young man alone
beside the hemmed-in sea.
The sky was holding back,
had gathered itself into itself,

refusing the relief of rain.
Years ago I stood
at the other end of Europe,
on Almeria's harbour wall,
heart swelled to bursting,

watched the sea go nowhere
and the sky hang dry.
Sometimes tears can't flow.
Dams hold back water.
We have nowhere to go.

Illumination

Basilica de Sta. Maria degli Angeli e dei Martiri, Rome

Mist has closed in this morning
reversing an early promise of blue sky.
Crows seek each other out,
birches stand unstirring,
dim ghosts caught out after light.

I close my eyes and play at praying
that the fog will lift, that when I look
again I'll see the trees relieved, focus
sharpened, height and depth restored
and all the garden's colours back.

Like that day in Rome, the vespas' drone,
cars fuming round the Piazza della Republica,
our senses dense and overloaded.
Then the felted thud of inner doors,
and us pitched, unsuspecting, into ether.

Fugitive

I have wrestled my way
through a tangle of clouds
into a dome
of Wedgwood blue.

Clay falls
from my fingernails,
a shower of brittle moons
under the pelting sun.

Leaves hold their own fire,
their embers burn,
brand the night sky.
The rage is mine.

In a Paper Cage

There are things in that wallpaper that nobody knows about but me, or ever will
– Charlotte Perkins Gilman, *The Yellow Wallpaper*

In those days it was wallpaper. Her eye
trapped in the pattern's maze, not wanting to
but following the stem up to the flower across

the trellis to the trailing roots above it
on the left. Always climbing upwards
as if their sun was calling them,

these deracinated creatures,
roots daddy-longleg-dangling
in thin air. So diagonally on

along the wall until she was cornered
and her eye ricocheted – flower, stem,
root this time – magnetically snared in

pointless exploration. On lucky days she caught
the pattern unawares and for as long as
she could hold her breath witches rode

on broomsticks, a tiger's face pressed
up against a fence. Ever since the need to break
the pattern, leave the pack,

bury deep her roots in loam.
Feel her stalk grow straight,
flowers open. Find her sun.

Ever since the magnet pulling,
uproot
uproot

Bifocal

Damp air moistens my cheeks,
rests lightly on my hair.
Boots sink into evening sand.
Oystercatchers scatter.

Through the acacia leaves
the square below
pants in the midday lull;
iron curtains clatter shut.

A homeless man unpeels
a nest of plastic bags,
hatches a book.
A child skateboards

diagonally into shadow.
Grey green flanks of Mweelrea
soft as antlers,
ribbon road unfurling.

Hillsides haemorrhage
into absence and longing.
Gulls over the Ramblas,
spectres in the night.

Flight Patterns

My wings hang pinned to the board
above my desk – between Mahon's
The Mayo Tao and a guide to making
compost – patient, limp white folds.
Under the oxters of their snowy promise,
black markings dance, the code to my next
foray. Not a short-haul weekend city break
but the well-worn arc of a patinated shuttle
plying back and forth to weave our lives
together. Darning holes.

Toll

The village chapel strikes the hour,
minutes later strikes the hour again.
Six short beats, like stick on iron.
Or twelve. Or two. You wait. And then
they come again, those tinny notes.

That morning, between eight and eight,
I travelled back across a restless night,
remembering how the screech owls
called as sleep refused to come. How
I'd heard twelve and twelve, both ones,

but neither twos. Still poised
between the eights, my mind tracked
forward to the day ahead, the return
journey, the long path
from one home to the other,

thinking that with time
you can get used to anything,
that being half in one place, half
the other, you are caught inside a clock
that strikes the hour twice.

LEFT LUGGAGE

This morning I woke with seawater
in my mouth. My eyes felt rinsed,
like after crying, my veins were
scoured, my limbs wrung out.
I was beached on a fogbound bed.
Adrift. Missing the aquatics.

Nothing is lost, just out of reach.
Everything that ever was, is –
somewhere – if only we can
get there, find the key, remember
the encrypted PIN, be brave enough
to jump. Know how to swim.

If only our feet have not been bound
at birth, our wings trimmed back
like wicks to suit our mothers, or
cobbled to a gooey mess by fathers,
confusing the discrete powers of
son and sun, deluded and controlling.

As long as no-one changed the locks
along the way and didn't tell us, or
dropped the keys or, worse still, built
a breeze block wall – a suicide bunker –
performing hara-kiri on our dreams. Left
bag and baggage rotting on the floor.

This morning I was reminded
by a taste of salt that we do not waste
those supine hours spent sprawled
unconscious in an oarless bed;
that we are all at sea, our time well spent
diving, back and back, to unpick locks, find home.

Prayer to a Night Train Driver

We have placed our lives in your hands,
invisible one, alone in your hallowed lair.
Lead us safely into night's dark maze,
along threads of steel to its core.

May sleepers lull us into childish slumber,
the tracks keep track of each and every dream.
Through silent suburbs glide us, past drowsy cows,
and sheep, heavy-coated under star-bent boughs.

O perfect stranger, in you we place our trust.
Spool in the ravelled fabric of our cares
and – clickety-clack, clickety-clack –
knit us whole into another dawn.

Above Castelnou

i.m. Nuala O'Faolain

Wild thyme was flowering,
and lavender
and dandelions bleached to lemon
by the sun. And wild roses –
everywhere – and crumpled purple cistus.

The hilltop was a shimmer
of electric blue
(some kind of cornflower)
and through it
every shade of pastel bloom.

And all along our way that day
tight yellow tufts of flowers
the French call *immortelles*.
Only the cuckoo-cuckoo
told a different story.

HIGH SUMMER

I saw a ship sail through a sea of grass,
the swell of seed heads heaving, the froth
of summer rising and clashing,
splashing against the landlocked hull.

I saw a farmer try to plough the sea,
setting the furrows lengthways to the shore,
turning, losing the traces, starting over,
the horses white and wild.

I saw the waves rise up, close over;
the grasses weave a curtain dense as brine.

Unsaid

for Yann

Silence can fill a room like an elephant,
its crosshatched bulk up against the wall,
sulking and seedy. Or it sits like a bird
in the breast of a child, ruffled and panting, afraid.

She used to be afraid of the black pool of silence
between them: the not-said, the almost-said,
the if-only-he-would-say-it. Words refusing to surface,
drawing her closer to the brink, wanting to plunge in,
to search them out herself.

Until he taught her how to peel her stare
from the centre of the pool, how to stay still,
to picture underneath the water fish turning
deep and green through liquid marble.

Tally Stick

Wood yields to the saw like chocolate,
surrenders to its snagging teeth,
accepts the fret and gnaw of metal,
a pile of dust its fate.

He lifts his stick like a scythe
to slash at thistles, I watch his arms,
how he starts to tick, a walking metronome
beating out a path, dead on time.

What if we decide to beat time too,
reverse the order, whittle us a tally stick
of love, some notches deep and flawless,
others splintered, new.

And letting off the ratchet, spin time backwards,
listen to the song our stick makes on the spokes.

Seeing

I think the best of life is life lived quietly where nothing happens
and the precious life is the calm journey through the day
– John McGahern, *Village Magazine*, 16–22 September 2005

A heron lands on a fence post above a stream,
getting it right with elegance,
smooth greys in harmony
with a distant tractor's rattle,
a hare tracing a line across a raggy field
where March gorse spills sunshine
in the Leitrim wilderness.

The heron lands on the fence post
single-minded and absorbed
in the precision of the moment.
There it sits, spare as bone,
quietly watchful, touches a still centre,
leaves us falling through ourselves
with wonder.

Zulu Beer Pot

I hold the comfort of your roundness
in my hands, cool heft of promise,

pregnant curves. I could be warming
wine, nursing beer or some concoction

brewed from nettle, lovage, lime.
A charm to bring on motherhood.

I listen with my fingers for new life,
small stirrings in your belly's depth,

a child's curled form, my palms
fine-tuned to pick up its first kick.

Green Road

Not a straight line through a forest,
luring two children on a pretext of shoes.
Mine has a bend that curves generously
to the brow of a hill of promise.
Stone walls lap the soft-bellied contours,
random telegraph poles coax the eye
from briar to bush.

On a distant motorway, or caught
in the chaos of my mind,
I can return there, call it up:
the gentle swerve, the poles, the hill's crest.
Eyes closed I can walk it,
my sinuous path to peace.

The Lake

The stones are sharp and green
under our luminous feet. We pick our way
into the lapping water until it's safe to flop.
We play at floating, sinking, bland water
spilling into our open mouths; we laugh
and splash, at home in our tea-brown lake,
until we remember it.

Trapped at the bottom of this mountain bowl
where hills bend over, link arms to keep it in,
where gorse and bracken wire the water's edge,
it turns in blind elliptic orbit, the phantom fish.

White limbs hang soft in the dark water now,
the monster's smooth firm skin can brush
against them, it can take a bite. And so we thrash
and choke our way back to our clothes,
scattered on the far-off shore. Our frightened feet
slide and tear on slimy stones. Biting our towels
we stand so small, eyes wide on the blank, black circle.

The Invisible Girl

You saw me as curtain, carpet,
the floral pattern of my dress
disappearing into background
like a lizard on a rock.

You thought I was 'just a child'
living in my childish head. You took
my silence for some sort of
absence, mistook me for my doll.

But my eyes saw, my ears heard,
my nose picked up
the layered scent of adult talk.
You paid no heed to the girl,

the pictures she was painting
on the inside of her skull,
how she smelt the rotting flowers,
could taste the brine of adult tears.

Sunday School

Fat words. Chocolate penny *talents*
shining round and gold; lush-leaved *bushels*

plump as Christmas puddings; and *prodigal,*
how it rolled and rolled around my mouth,

a glassy bull's-eye that never seemed to melt.
And then the bitter ones,

the words I wanted to spit out,
that snowman gone all wrong: *pillar of salt.*

I see it now, how drop by salty drop
the price of looking back is paid,

tears evaporate until there are no more,
crystals stiffen, the dripstone fattens.

A blessing for the child to see a snowman
consumed by flames she could not understand,

to recite a final prayer and then go home
where bright salt glittered in a dark blue bowl.

Cast Off

Under the thumb
of a great black glove I lie
pinned to the rancid pillow
of the bed my granddad died in.

Flattened by the vastness of the room
I wake to dark panes rattling
and the sound of my small universe
unravelling to a heap of wool.

I am ripped back to the last stitch;
the night itself spools back and back
until my skin dissolves, my bones
begin to melt. I shrink and sink

slowly into sleep again, see
my gran's grey needles lift, twelve stitches
safe. Click of bird feet, clink of bottles.
Light floods the room until I wake again.

May

Birdsong rescues me from frayed darkness,
stitches me back into the day.
Mayflower concentrates my dilute mind
with ivory buds as pure as babies' teeth.

PIVOTAL

The hardest journey is the journey home,
to make that horseshoe shape, slow
semi-circle, peel back from the otherness
of everything until you stare
into your own unblinking eye;
to unroll the fraying bolt,
heave it back onto the frame,
secure it to the hungry tenterhooks,
stretch it taut as goat hide,
be surprised to see the patterns
imperfections make.

Whale Watching

The lavender sea is giving nothing away.
We stand above the railway track
longing for those dark shapes
somewhere
down there
out of bounds
dark couplings
lumbering
loop into loop
slow wheels
heavy with future
ready to slew
the time come
fine spittle
into our
emptiness.

And then triumphally the two fingers,
a flippant send-up, held, then gone.

Black and White

Scientists Create a Black That Erases Virtually All Light
– *The Washington Post*, 20 February 2008

We've broken God's monopoly on the ineffable,
on blinding light, on a world without end, amen,
and us safe in the terminal building
waiting for Dad to collect us.

They've taken the white and made it whiter,
the light brighter,
and our children have clicked through their trapdoor,
are twirling out there in the blizzard,

arms probing in hope: of finding each other,
or another,
or something.
Snow-blinded in a world without maps. Amen.

They've taken the black and made it blacker,
ousted Satan, downgraded his gloom
– hardly dark enough to sin in –
to an elegant shade of grey.

You'll find God in the galleries,
gilt-framed, silver-bearded, with angels
harping on in their radiant robes and Christ
nailed to a cross.

Back in the real world we are all stumbling,
lured on through the whiteout
towards visions of perfection – fairytales
made from dreams

dreamt by bankers – dizzied by wilderness,
heading for chasms where the trap will fall open
and we'll be left
hanging.

A Perfect Shot

Heat cakes blood from red to brown.
Purple rings a child's eyes.
Her mother dies by candlelight.

If only snow would fall
or a big storm gather
I could turn away to the comfort of embers,
draw thick curtains,
unplug the small girl's lidless stare.

If only it would snow for me tonight
I could wake up to a new garden,
shapes changed and mysterious,
the leaves burdened and birds
picking through the icing for food.

Omission

Like butter it sits
on the tip of my tongue.
I do not speak.

Lorries drive through the night,
only the bushes cheer.
I turn over, look for sleep.

FELL

i.m. Jean Charles de Menezes, d. 22 July 2005

As I walked west from Dooniver Strand,
Slievemore broke through the bog,
thrusting through black butter,
scattering sundew, asphodel and heather
with its glistening fin.

And I thought of a Brazilian kitchen
when the worst news burst
through the flat sea of poverty,
policemen's peaked caps exploding
through white-washed walls.

The Gift

I send it straight into your head
to burrow there and to lay eggs

that, in time, will hatch and grow
and beat with angry wings for me.

I've wrapped it up in layers of brown
(they tell me you live in green)

and tied it all with skimpy string
I made from worn-out words:

faith, hope and charity; brother, sister;
solidarity. Ignore the buzzing –

it won't sting. Inside you'll find
a snake's sloughed skin, a stifled cry,

dust fine as ash, ash light as dust,
a trace of tears, some blood (quite dry)

and then a lot of empty space:
no water, food. No life.

DEPORTEE

Dread lodges in her ribcage
like a football.
Outside the holding room,
behind a sheet of ink,
tarmac laps the tyres
of sleeping planes.

One foot on it and she'll be lost,
sucked under its oily surface, black
waters closing over her brown skin
before the steely steps are reached.

The airport's mid-night silence
screams from neon walls; dead
corridors reverberate; tungsten
glares and kodachrome stares
irradiate her last flicker of hope.

The guards stand up.
The glass doors part.
Her foot touches the tarmac.
The football explodes.

Dragon's Teeth

January 2009, after the onslaught on Gaza

All week the sea spat rocks
onto the strip of road below;
loosed murderous missiles
under a black and cursing sky;
had ears only for the clack and smack
of its own stones, its battle-hungry roar;
exulted in a private orgy.

This morning the beaches lie exhausted
under a worn-out sky. Violence lingers
in the wreckage where sea birds
pick through shredded weed;
crows watch and wait on the fence
beside the road that is no more, eyes
turned from the simmering shame.

COUNTDOWN

Time to plant tears, says the almanac
– Elizabeth Bishop, 'Sestina'

It's not the iconic bear I care about,
though she looks sad. It's the ice
she's standing on that makes me want to shout

look! those bobbing, jaggèd lumps are the price
that's been agreed behind our backs,
dumping on our children's children the sacrifice

of their whole future. It's the end of almanacs,
of lying in the dappled shade of apple
trees, making love by musty haystacks

or the luxury we've enjoyed: to grapple
with age-old questions of eternity,
of which is best – temple, mosque or chapel.

Once water levels have risen and aridity
is here, we'll weep hot tears for our cupidity.

WITNESS

Not many saw the ruff of creeping froth
that lipped its way up sleeping cul-de-sacs,
slow-moving skim of water sheeting streets
the way a spring tide edges over sandy grass;
some stumbled onto unfamiliar sogginess
– workers leaving for an early shift –
felt the softness of a carpet waterlogged,
frowned briefly at the crystal sky;
rats ran, cats hunkered down to watch
the black tide climb; the moon
looked the other way.

And then it slid back down, discreet
as it had come, grass and asphalt clean
of any lick of silt. Next day the headlines
blazoned: *Slo-mo Tsunami Mystery,*
Gravity Defied, Sci-fi Horror Flood …
Priests cautioned against mass hysteria,
the president dismissed a terror plot.
But somewhere in the quiet turn of night
a woman filled three bottles. Assayed
three times, double-blind, three times the printout
read the same: *nothing to report*. The water
bore no history, content-free it came,
a message from the place where story ends.

DARKROOM

Floating up through the revealing liquid
a translucent ghost you come
on All Souls' Night,
my mother.

I grasp the tray and rock it back and forth,
searching your face,
wishing you peace,
washing the ripples from your brow.

Ground Floor Corridor, St James's Hospital

I'm sitting on a flip-up plastic seat. Waiting.
It's cornflower blue,
the blue of balloons.
The blue of hope. I wait.

The door that holds you in is powder blue.
Mist stretches and thins, letting the morning through
from snow-wrapped mountains.
My nostrils sting.

The floor's a beach, the sand-flecked tide
ebbed to polished mirage;
a fresh sluiced slab; a hall of mirrors
twisting faces into grief.

The trolley with the suction tubes
to make you come alive again
is red: fire brigade red, no-nonsense red, blood red,
just bled, not old or caked or brown. Or dead.

A white cloth drapes across the trolley top,
an altar sheet arranging its folds,
cornering the shadows, angling for attention.
Come and paint me. Now.

The exit doors are barred and midnight blue.
Too blue to be trusted.
I look back to the mountain sky.
Waiting. Watching the snow fall.

SURVIVAL

The jackdaws had begun to build
when I went in to set the fire,
a gift of kindling scattered
in the hearth. And through it

three metal tent pegs
six strips of wire
two covered lengths of flex
a fancy drawer handle
a child's blue plastic spade (broken)
some fencing staples
a heavy bolt
a ring pull
a strip of roofing felt.

'The lengths some creatures go
in order to survive', you kept
repeating, blind and bird-like
from your fireside chair.

While jackdaws heap up
ballast, you discard –
lightening, lightening –
in fierce and equal hope.

Waiting Room

Fear led him blindfold through veins and arteries,
groping his way along walls, into cavities and organs,
feeling for trouble.

Dread had her gimlet-eyed, Googling her way
into diseases unheard of, scrolling down symptoms,
clicking into nightmare.

Together they wait, panting and penned,
for the brand to strike, for the coin to land.

The Trees in Her Head

They grew slowly at first,
just one here and there.
It was the mess she objected to most,
twigs and leaves all over the place,
tap roots tripping her up, branches
catching at her clothes and hair.

The wood thickened,
it took away her light, her air.
She tried to pull it up, break it down.
Her hands tore.

When there was no way out
she grew quiet. Distant sounds
a bird
an airplane
children playing
bounced from leaf to leaf
into her hollow.

But sometimes a shaft of sunlight
cleaves the canopy, bathes a smiling girl.
Then she sees you, laughs,
and grips your hand.

Carapace

The gaff was in before I saw the second one.
I hooked the front crab's claw and
with a hollow crunch it locked itself
across the rock hole,
raised a pincer in defence
of both of them.

Without the innate skill of crabs,
awkwardly and sometimes tactlessly,
friends took turns to guard you,
raised pincers across the dinner table,
nipped comment in the bud,
locked claws around you until your shell grew back.

[OE BYRGAN]

I wanted to write about
the dimming light,
how our bones shift and sigh,
restless for warmth;
the way leaves yearn,
open their pores,
then open them more;

about bones lying like leeks
in green shrouds, gasping,
and the sun weighed down
by a pile of overcoats
thrown in a stack
at the back of the hill;

about the polyanthus and cowslip
that flowered in November
outside my back door,
how lonely they looked,
wrongly dressed for the season,
attracting the slimy kisses of slugs;

about blood running grey
and mould webbing human feet;
about how we bury bodies,
how down to earth it is.

Until I discovered the origins of our word
for putting someone in the ground
and that a string of US undertakers
had found the word as well
and liked it
and used it as their trade name
and that made me smile.

The Weight of Water

It could have been a beetle
(the light on its back)
until I saw how it moved.
That was the first day,
the first bud of water,
belly grown to bursting,
tracking its way
down the wall.

After that the weight grew,
bore down on my shoulder
hard against the dyke
where the wall darkened,
listened for the cue
to take me with it,
heels over head.

Nothing left to do
but hold my head clear,
latch eyes on a tree,
aim for it, manoeuvre
my limbs into a fork,
hope to win time,
to be spotted,
hauled to dry land.

Crossing

So we beat on, boats against the current, borne back
ceaselessly into the past
– F. Scott Fitzgerald, *The Great Gatsby*

If we are rowing into a future
behind our backs, watching the past
flow from us as we pull,
let me be heading for an island,
not upriver into a narrowing gorge
towards a source which may
or may not be there.

Better still, let me be standing
at a ferry's stern, laughing with
the frothing wake, lithe and slippery
on a buoyant sea. Stepping backwards
off the boat let my bag fall
between craft and quayside, compass,
watch and cellphone spilling through
the winnowed sand for crabs to tow away.

With time and space disposed of,
let me sit, my back against a boulder,
ringed round by fire of fuchsia
and montbretia as a pair of ravens
pass comment overhead. Or dangle
my legs from the cliff top's busy edge,
ducking the wooden wings of fulmars,
oblivious to the setting sun.

Diva

Words soar suddenly like startled larks,
their curved blades scissoring the sky,
shredding bolts of blue to deft mosaics.

Words trill in unrelenting song,
reeling out their story
until suddenly
it's done.

Photo courtesy of Lisa Molina

Geraldine Mitchell was born in Dublin and now lives near Louisburgh, Co. Mayo. In between she lived in France, Algeria, Spain and England where she taught English and worked as a freelance journalist. Previous books include two novels for young people, *Welcoming the French* (Attic Press, 1992) and *Escape to the West* (Attic Press, 1994), and a biography of Muriel Gahan, *Deeds Not Words* (Town House, 1997). She won the Patrick Kavanagh Poetry Award in 2008. In 2011 she was awarded a Bursary in Literature from the Arts Council, and in 2012 won the inaugural Poetry Ireland/Trócaire poetry competition. She is currently working towards a second collection.